SUPER SANDCASTLE
State Stories

RUPERT AND THE LIBERTY BELL

~ A Story About Pennsylvania ~

Written by Katherine Hengel

Illustrated by Bob Doucet

Consulting Editor, Diane Craig, M.A./Reading Specialist

ABDO
Publishing Company

Published by ABDO Publishing Company
8000 West 78th Street, Edina, Minnesota 55439.

Printed in the United States of America, North Mankato, Minnesota
112009
012010

 PRINTED ON RECYCLED PAPER

Editor: Katherine Hengel
Content Developer: Nancy Tuminelly
Cover and Interior Design: Anders Hanson, Mighty Media
Production: Colleen Dolphin, Mighty Media
Photo Credits: Peter Arnold Inc. (Jeff Greenberg), One Mile Up,
Shutterstock, Alan K. Wyand. Quarter-dollar coin image from
the United States Mint

The photo on page 8 was reprinted with permission of
Carnegie Mellon University, Pittsburgh, Pennsylvania. www.cmu.edu.

Library of Congress Cataloging-in-Publication Data

Hengel, Katherine.
  Rupert and the Liberty Bell : a story about Pennsylvania /
Katherine Hengel ; illustrated by Bob Doucet.
     p. cm. -- (Fact & fable: state stories)
  ISBN 978-1-60453-926-4
  1. Pennsylvania--Juvenile literature. I. Doucet, Bob, ill. II. Title.
  F149.3.H47 2010
  974.8--dc22
                              2009035422

TABLE OF CONTENTS

Erie

Allegheny
National Forest
(pg. 5)

Meadville

PENNSYLVANIA

Carnegie
Mellon
University
(pg. 8)

Punxsutawney

Appalachian
Mountains
(pg. 10)

Williamsport

Scranton

Allentown

Pittsburgh

Punxsutawney Phil
(pg. 19)

Altoona

Liberty Bell
(pg. 17)

Mason-Dixon
Line
(pg. 9)

ruffed grouse
(pg. 4)

Harrisburg

Somerset

Lancaster

MASON
DIXON
LINE

Gettysburg

Philadelphia

Fulton
Opera
House
(pg. 15)

white-tailed
deer
(pg. 12)

LEGEND

☆ CAPITAL   ● STORY START

○ CITY   --- STORY PATH

⋀ MOUNTAINS   ✷ STORY END

RIVER

Ruffed Grouse

The ruffed grouse is the state bird of Pennsylvania. Ruffed grouse live in the forest. They do not **migrate**. They spend most of their lives on the ground. They eat berries, seeds, and insects.

RUPERT AND THE LIBERTY BELL

Rupert the ruffed grouse lives in the Allegheny National Forest. He spends his days walking in the woods. He finds a lot of things to eat on the forest floor.

It's been a long winter for Rupert. He misses the sunshine and the mountain laurels. It's rare for a ruffed grouse to leave its home. But Rupert has had enough. "I am out of here!" he says. "Pennsylvania is all about liberty and independence. I'm going to spend the rest of the winter looking for the Liberty Bell!"

Allegheny National Forest

The Allegheny National Forest is in northwestern Pennsylvania. It covers more than 800 square miles (2,000 sq km). The Allegheny River runs along the west side of the forest.

5

Point State Park

Point State Park is in downtown Pittsburgh. The Ohio River starts there. The fountain in Point State Park sprays water up to 150 feet (46 m) in the air! The fountain is turned off during the winter. It comes back on in the spring!

Rupert decides to start his search in Pittsburgh. There are great universities there. Surely, someone at a university could help him! He follows the Allegheny River until he reaches Point State Park in Pittsburgh.

Rupert passes many theaters, **galleries**, and **restaurants** as he travels through downtown. He walks until he sees a sign for Carnegie Mellon University. "All right!" Rupert yells. He is proud that he found his way.

Pittsburgh

Pittsburgh is the second-largest city in Pennsylvania. It is often called "The Steel City." At one time, there were many steel companies there. Downtown Pittsburgh is shaped like a triangle. The Allegheny River and Monongahela River form two sides of the triangle.

Rupert arrives at the Carnegie Mellon **campus**. "It's beautiful here!" he says.

"We know!" a little voice squeaks. Rupert looks up. There are three squirrels on a branch above his head.

"Wow!" Rupert says. "You scared me! Usually I can hear squirrels moving around in the trees!"

Carnegie Mellon University

Carnegie Mellon University is in Pittsburgh. Andrew Carnegie founded it in 1900. Today, Carnegie Mellon University is ranked as one of the best colleges in the world!

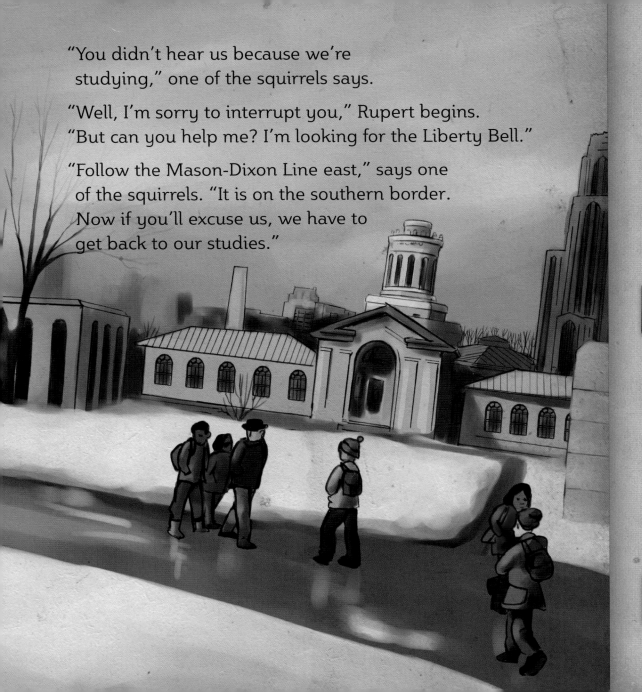

"You didn't hear us because we're studying," one of the squirrels says.

"Well, I'm sorry to interrupt you," Rupert begins. "But can you help me? I'm looking for the Liberty Bell."

"Follow the Mason-Dixon Line east," says one of the squirrels. "It is on the southern border. Now if you'll excuse us, we have to get back to our studies."

Mason-Dixon Line

Charles Mason and Jeremiah Dixon established the Mason-Dixon Line in the 1760s. It marked the border between the Maryland and Pennsylvania Colonies. The Mason-Dixon Line is 233 miles (375 km) long.

Appalachian Mountains

The Appalachian Mountains are almost 2,000 miles (3,200 km) long. They run along the east coast of North America. They are some of the oldest mountains in the world.

Rupert thanks the squirrels. "The southern border of Pennsylvania is a long way from home," he thinks.

Rupert decides to go for it. His friend William from summer camp lives in Gettysburg near the border. Rupert heads south and finds a Mason-Dixon marker. He follows the markers across the Appalachian Mountains.

MASON DIXON LINE

Rupert makes his way to Gettysburg National Military Park. It's a calm and beautiful place with many monuments. Rupert stops to admire the Soldiers National Monument. Then he sees William the white-tailed deer in the distance.

Gettysburg National Military Park

During the American Civil War, an important battle was fought at Gettysburg. After the battle, President Lincoln made a famous speech there called the Gettysburg Address. Gettysburg is now a national park. There are more than 1,600 monuments in the park.

White-Tailed Deer

The white-tailed deer is the state animal of Pennsylvania. It gets its name from the long, white hair under its tail. The males **shed** their antlers each winter. They grow new antlers in the spring.

"Rupert! You old ruffed grouse, you!" William says. "I can't believe you came all the way to Gettysburg!"

"I'm looking for the Liberty Bell," Rupert begins. "Do you know where it is?"

"No," William says, "But it has something to do with the American Revolution. You could probably learn more about it in Philadelphia. I'll go with you, but I need to stop in Lancaster first. It's on the way."

"Deal!" says Rupert. Then the two friends make their way through Amish country toward Lancaster.

Amish

The Amish people are known for their special **traditions**. They do not use electricity, cars, or other modern inventions. They are skilled at farming, **quilting**, and making things out of wood. Lancaster has a large Amish community.

13

Eastern Hemlock

The eastern hemlock is the state tree of Pennsylvania. It is an evergreen tree that can grow taller than 100 feet (30 m). Some eastern hemlocks have lived for more than 500 years!

14

Just outside of Lancaster, William stops by a huge eastern hemlock. "Here's my stop, Rupert. It's a family **tradition**!"

"What do you mean?" Rupert asks.

"Each year, I come here to **shed** my antlers. It's the same place where my father shed his antlers too."

"Wow," Rupert says. "How long has your family been doing that?"

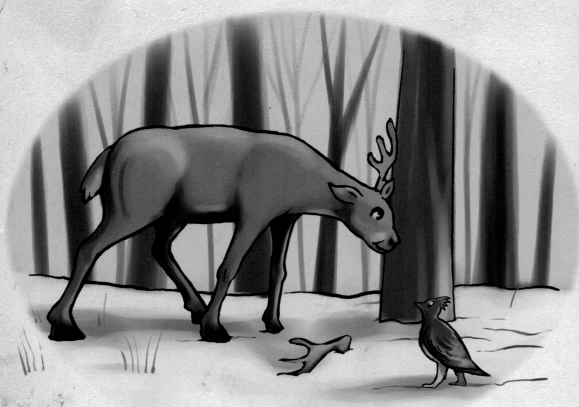

William stops to think. "My grandfather once said the **tradition** began the year that the Fulton Opera House opened. It's a theater in downtown Lancaster. We can walk by it on Prince Street."

The two make their way along Prince Street. "What a beautiful theater!" Rupert says.

Fulton Opera House

The Fulton Opera House is in downtown Lancaster. It was built where the old Lancaster jail used to be. It opened in 1852 and has been in business ever since! The Fulton Opera House is a National Historic Landmark.

15

Philadelphia

Philadelphia is the largest city in Pennsylvania. Its nickname is the "City of Brotherly Love." Philadelphia was an important city during the American Revolution. The Declaration of Independence was written and signed there.

The two friends make their way to downtown Philadelphia. "Look!" William says. "It's Greta the Great Dane from summer camp!" They cross the street to say hello. Greta gives them each a Philly cheesesteak sandwich.

"Thanks, Greta!" Rupert says. "We're looking for the Liberty Bell. Do you know where it is?"

"I sure do!" Greta says. She closes her stand and leads them to the Liberty Bell Center.

Philly Cheesesteak

½ green pepper, thinly sliced

½ onion, thinly sliced

2 teaspoons olive oil

½ pound roast beef, thinly sliced

salt and pepper

4 slices American cheese

2 hoagies, cut lengthwise

Preheat oven to 350°F. Sauté green pepper and onion in oil until browned. Remove from pan. Add roast beef to pan and season with salt and pepper. Cook until warm. Place two cheese slices in each hoagie. Stuff hoagie with meat mixture and wrap in aluminum foil. Place in oven for 5 minutes.

"There it is!" Rupert exclaims. "A **symbol** of liberty and independence. I can't believe I made it all the way here!"

"There are many **legends** about that bell," Greta says. "Speaking of legends, it's Groundhog Day! We should go to Punxsutawney!"

Liberty Bell

The Liberty Bell is an important symbol of U.S. freedom. There are many stories about how it got its crack. The truth is that the crack started small and grew over time. The Liberty Bell Center is in Independence National Historical Park.

17

Pennsylvania Firefly

The Pennsylvania firefly is the state insect of Pennsylvania. It is also called a lightening bug. It can make its body light up! That's how fireflies communicate with each other.

William and Rupert follow Greta to Punxsutawney. Thousands of happy people are celebrating there! Rupert asks the firefly next to him, "Why is everyone so happy?"

"Punxsutawney Phil the groundhog didn't see his shadow," the firefly says. "So spring is on the way!"

A ruffed grouse rarely flies. But Rupert is so happy that he explodes into flight. "What a day!" he exclaims. "I found the Liberty Bell *and* spring is coming! We'll be back in summer camp before you know it!"

THE END

Punxsutawney Phil

Punxsutawney Phil is a groundhog. There is a **legend** that he can tell how long winter will last. Each year on February 2nd, people gather to watch him come out of his hole. If he stays out, that means spring will come early. If he sees his shadow, that means winter will last six more weeks.

PENNSYLVANIA AT A GLANCE

Abbreviation: PA

Capital: Harrisburg

Largest city: Philadelphia

Statehood: December 12, 1787 (2nd state)

Area: 46,055 square miles (119,283 sq km) (33rd-largest state)

Nickname: Keystone State or Quaker State

Motto: Virtue, Liberty, and Independence

State flower: mountain laurel

State tree: eastern hemlock

State bird: ruffed grouse

State dog: Great Dane

State animal: white-tailed deer

State insect: Pennsylvania firefly

State song: "Pennsylvania" formerly "Hail Pennsylvania!"

STATE SEAL

STATE QUARTER

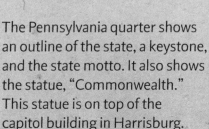

The Pennsylvania quarter shows an outline of the state, a keystone, and the state motto. It also shows the statue, "Commonwealth." This statue is on top of the capitol building in Harrisburg.

STATE FLAG

WHAT DO YOU KNOW?

How well do you remember the story? Match the pictures to the questions below! Then check your answers at the bottom of the page!

 **a.** groundhog

 **b.** white-tailed deer

 **c.** ruffed grouse

 **d.** eastern hemlock

 **e.** the Liberty Bell

 **f.** Philly cheesesteak

1. What kind of animal is Rupert?

2. What does Rupert want to find?

3. What kind of animal is Rupert's friend William?

4. What does William rub his antlers on?

5. What does Greta give Rupert and William?

6. What kind of animal is Punxsutawney Phil?

Answers: 1|c 2|e 3|b 4|d 5|f 6|a

What to Do in Pennsylvania

1 Visit the U.S. Brig *Niagara*
Erie Maritime Museum, Erie

2 Feed an Alpaca
Critter Country Animal Farm, Smithton

3 Tour the Capitol
Harrisburg

4 Learn about Chocolate
Hershey's Chocolate World, Hershey

5 Visit a Botanical Garden
Longwood Gardens, Kennett Square

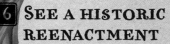

6 See a Historic Reenactment
Crossing of the Delaware, Washington Crossing

7 Ride a Hypercoaster
Dorney Park & Wildwater Kingdom, Allentown

8 Visit the Birthplace of Little League Baseball
Little League Museum, Williamsport

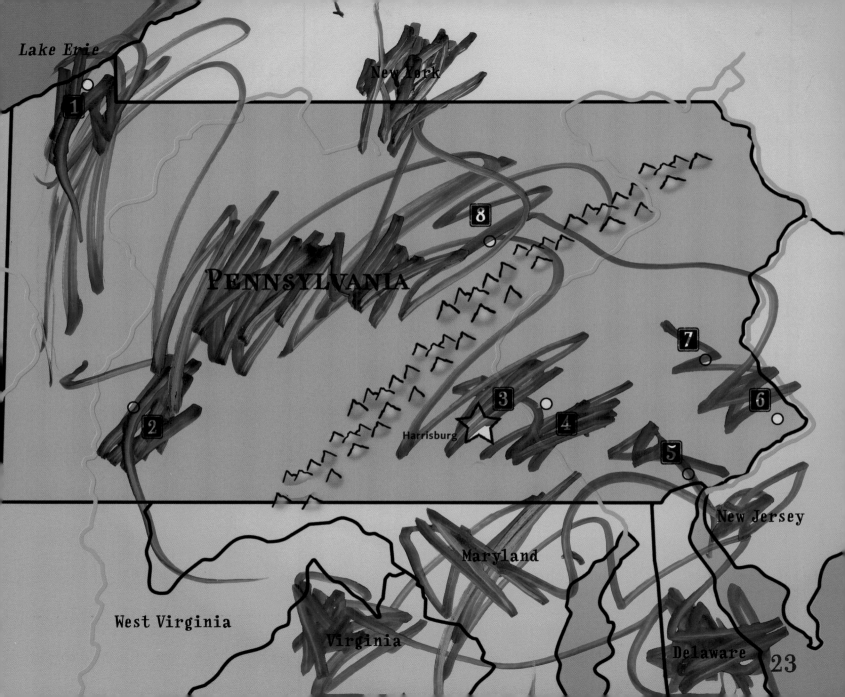

GLOSSARY

campus – the buildings and land that make up a college or school.

gallery – a place where art is displayed or sold.

legend – a story passed down through history that may not be true.

migrate – to move from one area to another, usually at about the same time each year.

quilt – to sew a blanket that has two layers of cloth with a warm filling such as wool or cotton in the middle.

restaurant – a place where people can buy meals.

shed – to lose something, such as skin, leaves, or fur, through a natural process.

symbol – an object that stands for or represents something else.

tradition – a custom, practice, or belief passed from one generation to the next.

24